Praise for *Albert Schweitzer: An Adventurer for Humanity*

by Harold E. Robles

"The contributions of Albert Schweitzer did not end with his death. The inspiration of his work will ripple on through mentees, generation after generation, for as long as humanity exists. Reading Dr. Albert Schweitzer's book *Out of My Life and Thought* while in a body cast at age fifteen not only helped me to develop a life philosophy—it also kindled an interest in both medicine and Africa. I welcome the re-publication of *Albert Schweitzer: An Adventurer for Humanity* by my dear friend Harold Robles, an exemplar of Dr. Schweitzer's concept of Reverence for Life. Harold has been a blessing for a new generation."

Dr. William Foege, recipient of the first Thomas Francis, Jr. Medal in Global Public Health, pioneered a successful strategy to eradicate smallpox in the 1970s. He is the former Director of the Centers for Disease Control and Prevention (CDC) and the Carter Center, and is a senior advisor to Bill and Melinda Gates. In 2012, President Barack Obama honored Dr. Foege with the Presidential Medal of Freedom.

Albert Schweitzer

Albert Schweitzer

An Adventurer for Humanity

Harold E. Robles

Preface by Rhena Schweitzer Miller

MAURICE BASSETT

Albert Schweitzer: An Adventurer for Humanity

Maurice Bassett
P.O. Box 839
Anna Maria, FL 34216

Contact the publisher:
MauriceBassett@gmail.com
www.MauriceBassett.com

Contact author Harold E. Robles: www.haroldrobles.nl

Cover design by David Michael Moore

Editing for second edition by Jessica Kempton-Jones & Chris Nelson

Layout by Chris Nelson

Photographs courtesy of Maison Albert Schweitzer: Archives Centrales Albert Schweitzer

ISBN: 978-1-60025-155-9

Library of Congress Control Number: 2020934659

Second Edition

To the children of the World, in particular my grandsons, Luca and Nico Robles, and my "bonus" grandsons, Harun and Tarik Ozturk.

May they find in the story of this great man a role model, held in high esteem, just as I did so many years ago.

And for my grandsons, whom I love dearly; I hope that they will come to understand the reason their Opa missed out on watching them grow up.

The author wishes to thank the following people for making the re-publication of this book possible:

Rhena Schweitzer Miller
(1919-2009)

Christian Will
(who passed away on my birthday, October 8, 2019)

Jessica Kempton-Jones

David Michael Moore

Michelle Nassau

Chris Nelson

My publisher and dear friend, Maurice Bassett

Contents

Preface by Rhena Schweitzer Miller   13

Chapter 1

The Adventure Begins   17

Chapter 2

How to Serve Humanity?   25

Chapter 3

Oganga   32

Chapter 4

Prophet in the Wilderness   42

Afterword by Christian Will   61

Sources   69

Important Dates   71

Further Reading   73

Index   77

A Call to Action   81

About the Author   85

I cannot but have reverence for all that is called life. That is the beginning and foundation of morality.

Albert Schweitzer

Preface

Rhena Schweitzer Miller

I am always amazed at the influence my father, Albert Schweitzer, has had, and still has today, on so many people. So often I meet medical doctors, ministers, musicians, and students who tell me that what they are doing is done under the influence of my father. Harold Robles is one of those who, while still a child, was deeply impressed by Schweitzer. His mother once told me rather sadly, "When he was eight years old I lost my son to your father."

What is the secret of this effect Schweitzer has on people? His range of talents was exceptional: philosophy, theology, and music were fields in which he excelled while still a young man. Leaving promising careers, following—as he said—his master, Jesus, he gave up worldly success to dedicate his life in direct service as a medical doctor to people in urgent need in Africa, which was then still "the dark continent." There, he found the principle of Reverence for Life, which became the basis of all his thoughts and actions and impelled him in later years to speak out in warning of the danger of nuclear testing and atomic warfare.

Many have listened to the voice of this man from the jungle. To know that he not only stood up for his beliefs in words and writing but also gave them concrete realization in his hospital in the African forest, gives him a unique credibility and authority.

Harold Robles has written this book about my father's life with enthusiasm and dedication. It is meant especially for young people. He feels compelled to share with them the enrichment my father has brought to his life and to make them aware of what just one person's actions can accomplish in our troubled world.

I hope that his enthusiasm will be contagious and communicate itself to his young readers.

Rhena Schweitzer Miller

Albert Schweitzer

Albert Schweitzer at age five.

Chapter 1

The Adventure Begins

Albert Schweitzer loved animals as much as people. One day when Albert was very young, a friend suggested it might be fun to go shooting birds. It was the last thing Albert wanted to do. But he was afraid his friend would make fun of him if he said no. Albert took up his slingshot and the two boys went out into a field.

They spotted some birds. Albert kicked lazily around on the ground for a sharp pebble. He picked one up and slipped it into his slingshot's band. He drew the band back and halfheartedly aimed at the unsuspecting birds where they perched.

Then something happened. Just at that moment, the bells of the nearby church rang out. Suddenly, the words that Albert had heard so often in that church flashed across his mind: "Thou shalt not kill."

Albert couldn't fire a shot.

He flung his slingshot into the grass. He shouted at the top of his lungs to frighten the birds into flight. Then, his eyes blurring with tears of shame and relief, he ran away.

Albert had made up his mind: Never, never would he kill for the sake of killing. His respect for living things was too strong. This respect or reverence turned into an idea Albert later called "Reverence for Life."

This idea guided Albert Schweitzer's life. It prompted him to become a great doctor, musician, and thinker. It also led him deep into the jungles of Africa to help the people living there. This is the story of Albert Schweitzer and the great adventure on which his "Reverence for Life" took him.

THE FIRST LOVE

Albert Schweitzer was born on January 14, 1875, in the little village of Kaysersberg in Alsace. Alsace lies between France and Germany. Today it is part of France, but at that time it belonged to Germany. A few months after Albert's birth, his father, Louis Schweitzer, a clergyman, was called to be a minister in the town of Gunsbach, about fifteen miles from Kaysersberg.

Albert's mother, Adele Schillinger, was the daughter of a pastor. Adele was a quiet woman with a powerful personality and a deep love of nature. Albert always felt her warmth and tenderness for him. She loved him dearly.

While still an infant, tiny Albert almost died. He suffered continuously from a high fever that no doctor could cure. Schweitzer later recalled: "On one occasion they actually thought I was dead, but the milk from neighbor Leopold's cow, together with the excellent Gunsbach air, worked wonders for me; from my second year onwards I improved marvelously, and became a strong and healthy boy, and in the house at Gunsbach I passed a delightful childhood with the companionship of three sisters and one brother."

In the town's small school, Albert became known as a dreamer with hardly any interest in schoolwork. Music was his first love. His father was his piano teacher. Schweitzer remembered the impact music had on him when he was young: "The charm of . . . songs thrilled me all over, to my very marrow, and similarly the first time I heard brass instruments playing together I almost fainted from . . . pleasure."

When he was eight years old and his legs were barely long enough to reach the pedals, Albert began to play the organ at the church in

The Schweitzer family in the garden of their Gunsbach home. From the left: Albert, his father Louis, his sisters Louise, Julie Adele, and Margerit, his mother Adele, his brother Paul, and the family dog Turk.

Gunsbach. It was this church whose tolling bells reminded Albert of his then unnamed idea of Reverence for Life.

FEELING AND LEARNING

When Albert was ten years old, he left home and went to live with his great-uncle Louis and great-aunt Sophie to begin his secondary education at a school called the Gymnasium at Mulhausen. His aunt and uncle were strict. Their lives were governed by the clock. They dictated certain times for piano lessons and practice, for homework, and for reading. They were extra-strict with Albert when it came to piano practice.

This made a chore out of what had once been a pleasure. So Albert made up his own music, or improvised, instead of learning to play properly. This frustrated his music teacher, Eugen Münch, to the point where one day he cried, "You don't deserve to have such beautiful music given you to play. If a boy has no feeling, I certainly can't give him any!"

But Albert had a deep love for music and was determined to prove it. Albert went home with the music for "Songs Without Words" by the German composer Felix Mendelssohn, and for a whole week he practiced the piece. When Albert played the music for his teacher, the teacher was so moved that he could only press the boy's shoulders in a gesture of pride and appreciation. There were no more accusations of lack of feeling.

Still, Albert did terribly in school. At the end of the school year, in the spring of 1886, he returned home with a report card so bad that there was doubt whether he would be allowed to return the next year. His parents did not scold him, but he was aware of their concern. If he were expelled, what would become of him?

Many years later, Albert Schweitzer recalled how one teacher made a difference in his life during the next school year. "A savior appeared for me in the person of a new [teacher], Dr. Wehmann." Dr. Wehmann had a tremendous amount of self-discipline and that impressed Albert. He became Albert's role model and the young student pushed himself to work harder each day at his studies.

Albert improved in school. History and science became his two favorite subjects. He became so strong in music that he decided to make it one of his subjects at the university. The other subjects were to be the study of religion, or theology, and the study of knowledge, or philosophy.

But before he could go to the university, Albert had to pass a stiff examination at the Gymnasium. Nobody thought the improved student would have much difficulty, but things nearly turned out disastrously—all because of a pair of trousers! On the examination day the young men in Albert's school dressed in their most formal clothes—usually a very long coat and black trousers. Albert had the coat, but lacked the black trousers. So he borrowed a pair from his uncle, who was much shorter. With pieces of string tied to his suspenders, Albert lowered the pants to the level of his ankles.

The result was ridiculous. The pants were baggy and drooped over Albert's shoes. Worst of all was the rear view. Albert's appearance caused uncontrollable laughter among his fellow students. The dean was outraged and decided to personally examine Albert, whom he thought was a joker. Albert was unable to answer many of the dean's difficult questions.

With things looking bleak, the dean turned to history. This was

Albert's favorite subject and his answers delighted the dean. Albert passed the examination and earned his diploma, with a special word of commendation from the dean. He had survived the tragedy of his trousers!

MUSIC AND STUDY

At eighteen, Albert enrolled as a student at University of Strasbourg. Late in the summer before entering the university, he received an invitation from his uncle Auguste and aunt Mathilde to visit them in Paris. He was very excited, and quickly accepted the offer. He had never before left his home province of Alsace.

Albert enjoyed Paris, with its big churches. One day he went with his aunt to visit the unique Cavaillé-Coll organ of the Church of Saint-Sulpice. This organ, named after its builder and considered one of the most magnificent in the world, is recognized for its matchless tone. At the church Albert's aunt introduced him to the famous organist and composer Charles-Marie Widor. Widor was in great demand as a music teacher. Normally he took only students from the Paris Conservatoire, a special music school. However, something about young Albert Schweitzer appealed to Widor. Maybe it was his playing, or it might have been Schweitzer's passion for the music of the great German composer Johann Sebastian Bach. Whatever it was, Widor made Albert Schweitzer a very proud young man when he agreed to take him as a pupil. Later, Widor and Schweitzer became close friends.

After school began, Albert divided his time between Strasbourg, where he studied theology and philosophy at the university, and Paris, where he worked with Widor. Within a few months, his studies were interrupted by military service, which was required of all young men Albert's age. Luckily, soldiering did not entirely interfere with his

This photo shows Albert when he was a student at University of Strasbourg.

studies. He was allowed to continue his education and attend lectures whenever his regiment was near Strasbourg.

When he had fulfilled his military duties, Albert returned to his studies. On May 6, 1898, he passed the examination for a degree in theology and then turned his energies to the study of philosophy. He was also about to take one of the most important steps of his life's adventure.

Chapter 2

How to Serve Humanity?

One day in 1896, while vacationing in his beloved Gunsbach, twenty-one-year-old Albert Schweitzer made the greatest decision of his life. He had been searching desperately for a meaningful way to devote his life to humanity. It seemed to him that he could not continue to enjoy such a happy life while all around him there was such sorrow and suffering as animals being mistreated and people everywhere living in poverty.

Albert took a sacred vow: He would continue to study theology, philosophy, and music until he was thirty years old. But from then on, to the end of his days, he would devote himself entirely to the service of suffering humanity.

He worked passionately. On a scholarship, he studied at Sorbonne University in Paris. There he was also able to resume his music training under his friend Widor. In a flurry of activity, Albert then returned to Strasbourg for his examination in philosophy, for which he was awarded a doctorate in 1899. He then journeyed to Berlin, the

Albert appears in this thoughtful pose around the time he
decided to devote his life to helping others.

German capital. There Schweitzer attended organ recitals and lectures on philosophy. A year later, on July 15, 1900, Schweitzer took his theological examination and received another degree in theology *magna cum laude*, a Latin phrase meaning "with great distinction."

While preparing for his theology degree, Albert Schweitzer was made a clergyman at St. Nicholas Church in Strasbourg. His chief responsibilities were to preach afternoon sermons and the Sunday children's service, and to teach confirmation classes. "To me preaching was a necessity of my being," he wrote later in his memoirs. "I felt it as something wonderful that I was allowed to address a congregation every Sunday about the deepest questions of life."

AN INNER STRUGGLE

Meanwhile, Albert struggled with his own personal question. He was only twenty-five years old, a learned man in music, theology, and philosophy. Still, he had not forgotten the promise he had made to himself when he was twenty-one. How to serve humanity was the question he asked himself over and over. There were orphaned, neglected, and abandoned children he could educate and care for. He could devote himself to the homeless, or help those just out of jail. All such work, however, required constant cooperation with welfare organizations, which meant red tape and too many rules, something Albert did not like and could not deal with. Deep inside he felt the urge to work in direct contact with those who suffered and needed help. But how could he be completely free to do it in his own way?

Sometimes, Schweitzer spoke about his inner struggle in the Sunday sermons he preached in St. Nicholas Church. He talked about how people seemed to have forgotten the difference between right and wrong and how they treated each other so badly.

Helene Schweitzer-Bresslau

AN ADVENTUROUS COMPANION

One day Schweitzer noticed a young woman who was always present at his sermons and the discussions about them after the service. They had met a couple of years earlier at the wedding of a mutual friend. The young woman's name was Helene Bresslau.

Helene was much inspired by Schweitzer's sermons, but she never spoke. So Schweitzer decided to challenge the silent watcher, and asked her how she enjoyed his sermons. "From the point of view of style, they leave much to be desired," she answered dryly, perhaps unwilling to demonstrate her interest in the young man. "Your German sounds . . . clumsy."

And so began the story of Albert Schweitzer and Helene Bresslau. She was a pretty, dark-haired woman whose father was a well-known Strasbourg historian. Originally, Helene had wanted to become a teacher. At eighteen she passed her examinations at the teachers' training college. In the autumn of 1902 she went to England to take up a position as governess, a woman who cares for and teaches children.

When she returned a year later, however, she had changed deeply. She became a full-time social worker for the town of Strasbourg, and founded a home for unwed mothers. She was so preoccupied with helping others that in January 1904 she began a course in nursing. Unknown to Albert, Helene Bresslau had also made a promise to herself to offer her life to the service of humanity. She, too, was in search of her destiny.

"My Search Was Over"

In the fall of 1904 Albert Schweitzer finally found his own answer to the question of how to serve humanity. He recalled: "I found on my table in the college in Strasbourg one of the green-covered magazines in which the Paris Missionary Society reported every month on its activities. I mechanically opened the magazine which had been laid on my table during my absence. As I did so, my eye caught the title of an article: 'The Needs of the Congo Mission.'"

The Congo referred to an area in central Africa that was at the time controlled by France. This region, also called French Equatorial Africa, comprised what are today the countries of Chad, Democratic Republic of the Congo, the Republic of the Congo. Gabon, and Central African Republic. The mission was a branch of the Catholic Church set up to teach the religion to the region's people and to help them. The article complained that there were not enough people to work in the mission. The article's writer appealed to those who followed Christ to offer themselves in this urgent work.

When Schweitzer finished reading the article, he recalled, simply: "My search was over." From that moment on, he would serve humanity by working in the Congo Mission. He would practice medicine in Africa.

Schweitzer immediately began preparing for his journey. He began studying medicine and took a course in tropical medicine in Paris. He received his M.D. certification, making him a doctor, in 1912. On June18 of that year, Albert and Helene were married. She had become a trained nurse and could assist him in his medical work. With his new bride, Albert moved to his parents' home in Gunsbach for the final months of preparation.

With his wife's help he compiled lists of drugs and medical supplies he estimated he would need for their stay in Africa. To raise the money to buy these supplies, Albert began giving organ concerts. He also asked family and friends for donations, a task he very much disliked. However, they had enough money by the end of that year and bought what they needed.

On a glorious Good Friday in 1913, Albert and Helene Schweitzer left Gunsbach by train for Bordeaux, France. The church bells that had startled the young Albert into realizing his reverence for life so long ago were ringing. The Good Friday service had just ended. Pastor Louis Schweitzer stood with his family on the small railway station platform to bid good-bye to his eldest son and daughter-in-law. The two were accompanied by seventy cases of medicines and medical supplies.

The Schweitzers poring over documents shortly before they left for Africa in 1913.

On Easter Sunday, on their way to Bordeaux, Albert Schweitzer had a chance to play the organ at Saint-Sulpice in Paris for the last time. When he finished, the Paris Bach Society, in appreciation of his many years as their organist, presented him with a piano with organ pedals attached to it. The piano itself was encased in a lead-lined crate to withstand the humid tropical climate of Africa. The same day, the Schweitzers left for Bordeaux, where the steamship *Europe* waited to carry them to Africa.

Chapter 3

Oganga

As Albert and Helene set sail for Africa, the dark clouds of war were about to gather over Europe. In a little more than a year, an assassin's bullet would fell Franz Ferdinand, Archduke of Austria-Hungary. The murder would pit France, Great Britain, Russia—and, eventually, the United States—against Austria-Hungary and Germany in the twentieth century's second most devastating military conflict, World War I. Even in remote Africa, the war would touch Schweitzer's life.

The sea journey was stormy as well. The ship rocked on the waves for weeks on end. Most of the passengers were sick, but not Albert. He spent hours in daily conversation with a specialist in tropical medicine he had met aboard the ship. It was this specialist who warned Schweitzer to never take one step in Africa without a hat. Unprotected exposure to even a few minutes of the African sun could be dangerous. Schweitzer never forgot this warning.

While almost everyone on board was worn out by the long and uncomfortable trip and could only manage a feeling of relief when the ship finally arrived at the Congo's Cape Lopez on Monday, April 14, 1913, Albert Schweitzer was overjoyed.

WATER MIRRORS AND MONKEY TAILS

The journey, however, was not over. The final destination was Lambaréné (pronounced lam-BAH-reh-neh), an island in the middle of the Ogowe River in a region of west Africa that is now the country of Gabon. To reach Lambaréné, Albert and Helene had to sail up the Ogowe on a riverboat.

The boat was broad and shallow. Two wheels at the back propelled it. When high tide covered the sandbars at the river's mouth, Albert, Helene, and their African crew embarked.

Years later Albert Schweitzer recalled his astonishment at first seeing the Ogowe and the flooded forest along its banks: "Who can really describe the first impression they make? We seemed to be dreaming! It is impossible to say where the river ends and the land begins, for a mighty network of roots, clothed with bright-flowering creepers, projects right into the water. . . . In every gap in the forest a water mirror greets the eye; at every bend in the river a new [stream] shows itself. . . . then—yes, there can be no mistake about it!—from the branch of a palm there hang and swing—two monkey tails! Now the owners of the tails are visible. We are really in Africa!"

As the river narrowed, the current strengthened. It took another day before the Schweitzers finally glimpsed Lambaréné.

LAMBARÉNÉ

Lambaréné was one of four mission stations run by the Paris Missionary Society along the Ogowe River. There had been no doctor in the area for many years. As soon as the Schweitzers arrived, news spread through the jungle that an *oganga*, a healer, had come to take away the people's sickness.

The Paris Missionary Society had promised Schweitzer a little bungalow to use as a temporary hospital. But there was no hospital waiting for him. He searched for somewhere to work that would be sheltered from the sun and the frequent tropical rainstorms. The only place was an old chicken coop, which had been built by a former missionary. It was better than nothing.

For many days all hands at the little mission were hard at work bringing the heavy cases of medical supplies up the hill from the river. The floor was cleaned, the walls scrubbed and whitewashed, and shelves installed. An old cot served as the first operating table.

The Schweitzers were in business, and faced the next problem. Every tribe in the area spoke a different language. How were they to understand them all and how could they be understood? A lucky discovery brought the answer. A man named Joseph Azvawami arrived one day as a patient in the hospital. He had been working as a cook for European settlers but had lost his job because of ill health. Joseph could speak French and knew many of the African languages. Although he could not read or write, Joseph quickly learned how to tell medicines apart from the shapes of the letters on their labels.

To his new job as medical assistant to Dr. Schweitzer, Joseph brought a colorful touch. He referred to human body parts in the language he used in his former job as a cook. He would say, "This man

The former chicken coop that served as both a house and a hospital for the Schweitzers when they arrived in Lambaréné. Chicken wire still surrounds the outside of the building in this photo.

His first year in Lambaréné, Schweitzer performed all surgery in this makeshift operating room.

has pains in his right leg of mutton." Or, "This woman has pains in her upper left cutlet and in her filet."

The variety of the diseases and illnesses shocked Dr. Schweitzer at first. From miles around came people suffering from malaria, severe diarrhea, ulcers, hernias, the dread sleeping sickness spread by tsetse flies, and leprosy. Larger quarters were needed to house some of these patients. They would need constant care.

The Schweitzers several months after their arrival at Lambaréné. This photo shows they hadn't forgotten the advice of the passenger aboard the *Europe*: "Never take one step in Africa without a hat."

Slowly, however, a way of caring for everyone emerged. During operations, Mrs. Schweitzer took care of the instruments, gave patients the drugs that put them to sleep for surgery, and assisted her husband every step of the way. She also distributed food and supervised the washing of the linen and bandages. Nothing in Lambaréné was ever thrown away; bandages were washed, disinfected, and used over and over again.

To relieve the tension after a hard day's work, Dr. Schweitzer played the piano given him by the Paris Bach Society. As the music of Bach, Mendelssohn, and Widor poured from the little house and filled the jungle night, the tension and pressures of the day drained from the tired shoulders of Albert Schweitzer.

House Arrest

In this place where time seemed to stand still, the doctor and his wife took little note of the world they had left behind. However, mail from Europe soon brought terrible news. In August 1914, war had broken out between Germany and France.

At that time, Gabon was controlled by France. Schweitzer was born in Alsace, which then belonged to Germany. Because he was a German living on French soil, the French government declared him an enemy. French officials placed Albert and Helene under house arrest. They could not leave the hospital at Lambaréné. Worst of all, they were forbidden to treat their patients, who desperately needed their care.

For the first time in his adult life, Albert Schweitzer had too little to do. He remembered, however, that for a long time he had wanted to write a book about how the ways in which people lived and treated each other had grown worse. But he had not been able to find the necessary

The Schweitzers expanded their quarters in Lambaréné, as seen here. But their improved house became their prison: They were under house arrest around the time of this photo.

time. Now he had the time and it was clear to him that people everywhere had taken a turn for the worse.

On the second day of house arrest, Schweitzer set to work on the book, called *Philosophy of Civilization*. As he had done so often before, Schweitzer asked himself many questions: Why did humanity murder and destroy? Was there a key to understanding life? The books on religion and philosophy he had read were filled with beautiful and noble principles such as "Thou shalt not kill." Why did those great ideas fail to inspire human beings? Schweitzer struggled, often despairingly, to answer these colossal questions. Often, he mused, animals treated each other more humanely than humans themselves. They never killed each other unless they were in need of food, or when forced to defend their young.

At times it seemed to him that the answers were near, and yet he said he felt as if he were "leaning with all my weight against an iron door which would not yield." For weeks Schweitzer pondered his questions as he sought to find the words and phrases to express what he felt in his heart.

Meanwhile, Widor and others in Europe worked for Albert and Helene's release. Finally, in late November 1914, the French government in Africa lifted the house arrest. The Schweitzers could travel and, most importantly, continue their work.

REVERENCE FOR LIFE

Although Schweitzer gladly returned to caring for his patients, the monumental questions he had posed for himself during his house arrest still troubled him deeply. In September 1915, he was summoned to see the ailing wife of a missionary who lived far away. He made the long journey on a riverboat. Schweitzer sat on the boat's deck, which was crowded with people. He was lost in thought, straining to solve the problems that so disturbed him.

Then one day on the journey, he recalled, something happened: "At sunset of the third day, near the village of Igendja, we moved along an island set in the middle of the wide river. On a sandbank to our left, four hippopotami and their young plodded in our direction. Just then,

A view of the Ogowe River. While journeying on this river, Albert Schweitzer conceived the idea of "Reverence for Life."

in my great tiredness and discouragement there flashed upon my mind . . . the phrase 'Reverence for Life.' The iron door had yielded: The path in the thicket had become visible."

Seeing the humble hippos caring for their young helped Schweitzer realize something about why so many people mistreated each other. They did not *care* for each other. Only by caring for and respecting each other, having reverence for life, could people treat others—and all living creatures—better.

From that day forward, for all the days of his life, he would devote himself to the preservation of life. The idea of Reverence for Life became the key that Albert Schweitzer had sought to open minds and hearts, to cure humanity.

However, not everyone shared Schweitzer's desire to cure humanity. In Europe the war raged on. A new order from the French government arrived. All enemy aliens were to be transferred to France. There they would be held in prison camps for the duration of the war.

Tired and weary of yet another interruption of their urgent work, the Schweitzers packed their belongings and stored the medical supplies in sheds. They bid many sad farewells to the patients and workers at the mission and boarded a river steamer. Oganga, the healer, was leaving the people he had come to help. It was a time of great sorrow, for who knew when he would come back as he had promised?

On the sea journey to France, the Schweitzers were under constant guard and were forbidden to have any visitors. To occupy his mind and to make full use of his time, as usual, Albert Schweitzer began to work. But how? There was no place for a table in the small cabin. So he decided to learn by heart some of Bach's music and Widor's Sixth Organ Symphony. He used the top of one of his storage trunks as an imaginary organ keyboard and pressed imaginary pedals on the cabin floor. And the beautiful, immortal music played in his imagination. The inner concert prevented Dr. Schweitzer from brooding over the dark future that lay ahead.

Chapter 4

Prophet in the Wilderness

At last the ship arrived in Bordeaux, the French port from which the Schweitzers had sailed four years earlier. There they and other prisoners of war were kept in a temporary barracks called the Caserne de Passage, before being assigned to prison camps.

The Schweitzers were taken to a prison camp called Garaison in France's Pyrenees Mountains. The prison in Garaison was an old, cold former monastery with a high-walled courtyard and long rambling corridors. Albert came down with severe diarrhea, and Helene was stricken with a recurrence of tuberculosis, the lung disease from which she had suffered as a young woman. Among all the people with trades and professions at Garaison, there was only one physician: Albert Schweitzer.

Despite his illness, Schweitzer went to work in the prison practicing medicine and even dentistry.

In March 1918, the Schweitzers were transferred to yet another camp, this one at St. Remy. Here, Dr. Schweitzer was allowed to assist the pastor and he often preached sermons. But St. Remy did not agree with the Schweitzers. Both of them became so ill and weak that in July they were told that they would be sent back home to Gunsbach.

They were not even strong enough to carry their little bit of luggage to the train. In Gunsbach, Schweitzer recovered, but for the rest of her life Helene would have to live with the aftermath of the tuberculosis.

All their dreams seemed to have come to nothing. The violence and hatred of war were becoming too much for this sensitive couple. During the past four years, moreover, they had endured not only house arrest and imprisonment, but grief: Albert's mother had been trampled to death by a cavalry regiment in 1916.

There was, however, a ray of hope: the birth of their daughter, Rhena, on January 14, 1919, Albert Schweitzer's forty-fourth birthday. Rhena was named by her father in honor of the River Rhine in Germany.

No matter what happened in his life, Schweitzer's thoughts returned time and again to his jungle hospital in Lambaréné. He decided to use all his energy to secure the money necessary to go back to Africa to resume the task he had started. But there was little hope. Schweitzer recalled: "Ever since the war I had felt rather like a coin that has rolled under a piece of furniture and has been forgotten there."

In December 1919, however, Schweitzer received an invitation

Young Rhena with her father in Gunsbach.

Sitting at the organ in Holland. During the 1920s, when this photo was taken, Schweitzer played concerts throughout Europe.

from Archbishop Nathan Soderblom to deliver a series of lectures at the Uppsala University in Sweden. Archbishop Soderblom had known Schweitzer and remembered him as a promising young theologian and philosopher. He had followed Schweitzer's career with great interest.

The lectures marked a turning point. His final lecture was devoted to the concept of Reverence for Life. His audience was enthusiastic. Later Schweitzer wrote: "I found for the first time an echo to the thoughts I had been carrying about with me for the last five years." Perhaps the world was prepared to hear his message.

Besides the lectures Schweitzer gave at the university, he found that people were interested in his work in Africa and asked him to speak about it. He gave lectures about Lambaréné and also organ concerts. He soon realized that he could earn money this way and possibly return to Africa.

Archbishop Soderblom also encouraged Schweitzer to write a book about his African experience. In 1921, Schweitzer wrote *On the Edge of the Primeval Forest*. The book was translated into many languages, bringing him considerable renown and large sums of money. He could now repay his friends the money he had borrowed, and make plans to go back to Africa.

The decision to leave, however, was not an easy one. Helene could not go back with him. She had not fully recovered from tuberculosis and she now had little Rhena to look after. Helene knew as well as anyone just what dangers and hardships her husband would face upon his return to Lambaréné. But she let him go; she even encouraged him. She had always put the cause first. No sacrifice was too much for either of them.

OGANGA RETURNS

Accompanied by a young English college student, Noel Gillespie, Albert Schweitzer returned to Africa in April 1924. The news of his arrival traveled like wildfire. Everyone was overjoyed and Schweitzer's excitement was great.

But what had become of his hospital? The jungle had reclaimed

The doctor in his other "career" as a builder. This photo shows Schweitzer supervising construction of his new hospital.

much of the little clearing that he and Helene had left seven years before. The doctor and Noel set to work, and after many months of labor, managed to return the hospital to its previous state. During that time, Schweitzer was a doctor in the morning and a carpenter in the afternoon.

A year later, two doctors and two nurses arrived from Europe to become members of Schweitzer's hospital staff. It soon became clear that a new, larger hospital was needed. There was no room for expansion at the present site.

Two miles upstream Schweitzer found the perfect spot to build his new hospital. The local authorities granted the doctor nearly two hundred acres of land. Weeks of exhausting labor turned into months, and the months into more than a year. On January 21, 1927, part of the new hospital was finished and patients were transferred from the old one. There was now room for two hundred patients and quarters for the hospital staff.

AN ANIMAL HAVEN

Schweitzer's new hospital was not only for sick people. It was also a haven for animals. From near and far, sick, old, and wild animals found their way to the Albert Schweitzer Hospital. Sick animals were nursed to health until they were well enough to return to the jungle. Having tasted life with Schweitzer, however, some of the animals chose to stay.

Schweitzer was always surrounded by animals. It was as if they knew that with him they were safe. And how right they were! Everyone in Lambaréné shared the doctor's belief that all life was sacred, including the lives of insects. Schweitzer had a special private circle of animals. There was Caramba the dog, Anita the antelope, Parsifal the pelican, and Sisi the cat.

These photos show Schweitzer later in life among the citizens of the animal haven. Here he writes a letter under the supervision of a faithful dog . . .

. . . and admires a pelican, perhaps a friend or relative of Parsifal, or even Parsifal himself.

WORLD FAME

Fame was beginning to catch up with Albert Schweitzer. From all over the world requests for organ recitals and lectures poured in. He traveled regularly to Europe and elsewhere. In churches and in universities Schweitzer explained what he meant by Reverence for Life. His words, his bright face, his modesty—but most of all his heartwarming sense of humor—moved people everywhere. More and more people called him a "Prophet in the Wilderness" once they understood his ideals and principles. Many followed him into service in Africa and elsewhere throughout the world.

Awards, honorary degrees, and many articles of praise came. *Life* magazine named him the greatest man in the world. His books became best-sellers, and he became a touchstone, an inspiration for a whole generation. During these next years Albert Schweitzer lived a busier life than most men half his age.

WORLD WAR II

In 1939, Schweitzer again traveled to Europe, where he intended to work on new books. He had hardly set foot on French soil when he realized that World War II was on the point of breaking out. He had anxiously followed the rise to power of German dictator Adolf Hitler, whom he considered a threat to humanity and to world peace.

Schweitzer made up his mind immediately. His place was in Lambaréné. He took the same ship back to Africa. Mrs. Schweitzer and Rhena went to Switzerland—a traditionally neutral country—where they would be safe.

In August 1941, however, what Dr. Schweitzer himself described as a near miracle occurred. A bus arrived in Lambaréné and aboard was Mrs. Schweitzer! Somehow she had managed to get to Lambaréné, via Switzerland, France, Portugal, and Angola. She realized that her husband was in need of all the help he could get, so she left Rhena (who

Albert Schweitzer at his piano in Lambaréné. He took breaks from his demanding schedule by filling the jungle with music.

was by then an adult) in Switzerland, and joined her husband. They were overjoyed to see each other again. For many long years during the destruction of World War II, Albert Schweitzer remained in the jungle, devoting himself entirely to the care of the sick.

OPENING EYES

In the summer of 1949, Dr. and Mrs. Schweitzer made their only visit to the United States. They arrived by ship on June 29 in New York. Dr. Schweitzer had been invited to give an address for the celebration of the two-hundredth birthday of the German poet and writer Johann Wolfgang von Goethe in Aspen, Colorado.

He was offered a large sum of money for his speech. With this amount, he would purchase a large supply of a new American drug to fight leprosy. Many people came to Schweitzer's hospital afflicted with the terrible disease, which caused deforming lumps on their skin and paralyzed their muscles.

All through his life Schweitzer had studied the works of Goethe and had gained much from the thinking of this world-minded poet and writer. He pointed out in his lecture that Goethe was a keen observer of evil in humanity and in society. Yet he also stressed Goethe's belief in doing good for the pure love of good rather than for personal gain.

Before leaving Aspen, Dr. Schweitzer spoke simply of his own beliefs during an interview: "What the world lacks most," he said, "is men who occupy themselves with the needs of other men. In this unselfish labor a blessing falls on both the helper and the helped. . . . Our greatest mistake as individuals is that we walk through life with closed eyes and do not notice our chances. As soon as we open our eyes

This photo was taken at Schweitzer's lecture in Aspen, Colorado. He poured
his heart into his talk and impressed people throughout the
United States during his one brief visit.

and deliberately search, we see many who need help—not in big things, but in the littlest things. Wherever a man turns he can find someone who needs him."

Schweitzer found that his idea of Reverence for Life appealed to Americans. He recalled of his trip: "On my visits to cities and universities, I also found that my teachings were the objects of deep interest."

THE NOBEL PEACE PRIZE

Returning to Africa in the fall of 1949, Dr. Schweitzer immediately began plans to establish an entire community in his hospital to help leprosy patients. He still needed a large sum of money, however, and he was gravely concerned over where it would come from. One answer came in the form of a Peace Prize awarded to him by the German Association of Publishers.

Another answer came in 1952 when Albert Schweitzer was awarded one of the world's greatest honors, the Nobel Peace Prize, for his efforts on behalf of the brotherhood of nations. At that time, Schweitzer was in Africa. His nephew, who was with him, was the first to hear the great news over the radio. It was late in the evening, but he rushed into his uncle's room and without any explanation enthusiastically congratulated him. Schweitzer, whose humble mind thought immediately of his animals, grinned: "So finally it has happened. My black cat has had her kittens! That is splendid!"

It is customary for Nobel Prize winners to travel to Norway to receive the prize in a solemn ceremony. An exception was made for Albert Schweitzer. The seventy-seven-year-old doctor was too busy working in his jungle hospital to make a special trip. In November 1954,

The hospital in Lambaréné, shown here in the 1950s, grew steadily. Schweitzer put the money he earned from his awards, lectures, and writings into its expansion.

however, Dr. and Mrs. Schweitzer traveled to the city of Oslo to receive the Nobel Peace Prize from the hands of King Haakon of Norway.

Following the official ceremony, Dr. Schweitzer delivered a wonderful speech. He took the opportunity to make a powerful plea for peace. At the end of World War II the world had witnessed the horror of nuclear war when the United States used the atomic bomb against Japan. Schweitzer spoke of how millions of men and women now lived in fear of nuclear war. He warned that a nuclear war could destroy far more than men and women. It could wipe out the entire planet. Schweitzer pleaded for greater compassion not only for human beings but for all living things. His opposition to nuclear weapons stemmed from his total reverence for life.

A NEW CHALLENGE

The Nobel Prize not only brought the doctor the great honor he deserved, but also a fine sum of money. He could now fulfill his dream of building a village for his leprosy patients.

While some might have viewed winning the Nobel Prize as the climax of a life's work, Schweitzer saw it as a new challenge—to work for world peace. He became obsessed with efforts to stop nuclear bomb tests and the preparation for new wars.

Norman Cousins, a prominent American editor and a leader in the fight against the nuclear danger, came to visit Dr. Schweitzer in Lambaréné in 1957. He urged Schweitzer to take an even stronger stand on the issue. Cousins was able to persuade Dr. Schweitzer to speak out in a radio appeal called a "Declaration of Conscience" via Radio Oslo, a station in the city in which he had received the Nobel Peace Prize.

This was followed in 1958 by three worldwide appeals, again via Radio Oslo. These appeals were later published in a book entitled *Peace or Atomic War?*

During these years, Schweitzer's goal was to bring about a safer world by persuading governments to give up nuclear weapons and nuclear testing. He was partially successful. In 1963, Great Britain, the

Schweitzer also set up programs to help people help themselves. People from Lambaréné line up to receive food they can prepare for their sick relatives at home.

Soviet Union, and the United States signed a limited agreement banning nuclear tests. The agreement, called the Limited Test Ban Treaty, was the result of, among other things, Schweitzer's efforts. President John F. Kennedy wrote to thank him for inspiring support for the successful conclusion of the treaty, calling him "one of the transcendent moral influences of our century."

Meanwhile, honors, awards, and many honorary degrees were given to Schweitzer. In 1955, he was invited to London, where, at Buckingham Palace, Queen Elizabeth II invested him with the highest honor the British Crown can bestow—the British Order of Merit.

In 1957, Helene Schweitzer died in Zurich, Switzerland. Her ashes were buried in the little cemetery at the Lambaréné hospital. In 1959, Albert Schweitzer made his last trip to Europe. Upon his return to Lambaréné he decided to remain in Africa for the rest of his life. Many great men and women came to pay him honor. He corresponded and wrote books and many articles. He cared for his patients and animals, and as often as he could played his beloved Bach.

As he neared his life's end, Schweitzer said of those he had known who had died:

> When I look back upon my early days I am stirred by the thought of the number of people whom I have to thank for what they gave me or for what they were to me. At the same time I am haunted by a [painful knowledge] of the little gratitude I really showed them while I was young. How many of them have said farewell to life without my having made clear to them what it meant to me to receive from them so much kindness or so much care! Many a time have I, with a feeling of shame, said quietly to myself over a grave the words which my mouth ought to have spoken to the departed, while he or she was still in the flesh.

Burning the long candle late into the night. This photo shows Albert Schweitzer, working at his desk in Lambaréné.

Perhaps it was a signal that he knew his own end was near. His friends pleaded with him to come back and to settle in his native country. Had he not earned a well-deserved rest? "You cannot burn a candle at both ends," they said. "Yes," Schweitzer replied, stretching himself to his six-foot height, "you can, if the candle is long enough."

On September 4, 1965, however, the candle that had burned so passionately went out. Dr. Albert Schweitzer died at his hospital in Lambaréné. He was ninety years old.

Afterword: Harold Robles & the Power of Albert Schweitzer's Example

Christian Will

Albert Schweitzer's work in Africa, as well as his philosophy of Reverence for Life, has lasted for many years, long after his death. Today, in Lambaréné, a new hospital with running water and electricity has been built behind the one that Schweitzer first built in 1913. In the old hospital, Albert Schweitzer's room has remained just as he left it, becoming a museum for the many visitors who flock each day to see where this great doctor once lived, worked, and practiced his Reverence for Life.

Other hospitals bearing Albert Schweitzer's name have been built in Mexico, the Netherlands, Korea and Brazil, to name just a few. Schools and relief organizations to help the sick and the needy have been established all over the world—all named after the man who loved the sound of human laughter just as much as he loved the music of Bach.

The Albert Schweitzer hospital in Lambaréné was dedicated in 1981.

The man remembered as the "Prophet in the Wilderness" left behind a legacy that must not die. Schweitzer's thoughts, his words, and above all, his modesty must be passed on, like a flaming torch, from generation to generation. That is precisely what the author of this superb book, my dear friend Dr. Harold Robles, has been doing for as long as *he* has lived. Well, to be precise, from the tender age of just eight years old.

When I think of Harold and his dedication to humanity, I am

reminded of Albert Schweitzer's own spirit. As the great American author and world peace advocate Norman Cousins once said:

> The greatness of Schweitzer, indeed the essence of Schweitzer, is the man as symbol. It is not so much what he has done for others, but what others have done because of him and the power of his example.

Harold Robles does just this. Not only does he do good for those around him, but he also encourages others to do the same.

At school, Harold created the Albert Schweitzer Youth Club, which raised money to support the Schweitzer hospital in Lambaréné, West Africa. Although after school he studied business management, his love always belonged to public health and education. Harold's main interest lay in finding successful ways to provide health education to the poor. As time went on, he began to understand that healthcare education and information would help him carry out his version of a Reverence for Life. Harold began to consider health education as a basic human right. It was with this idea that Harold began to shape his life's work.

In 1973, Harold started the Albert Schweitzer Center in the Netherlands. Two years later he was appointed Secretary General of the International Schweitzer Organization (ASIL), an organization founded by Dr. Albert Schweitzer in the 1930s. In 1978 Harold moved to the United States, where he worked for the Red Cross. Harold became a U.S. citizen in 1990.

In 1984, Harold, together with Albert Schweitzer's daughter, Rhena Schweitzer Miller, started the Albert Schweitzer Institute for the Humanities (ASIH). The ASIH is a non-profit organization dedicated to advancing the philosophy, ideas and humanitarianism of Dr. Albert Schweitzer through action, research, education and publication. During Harold's time there, the ASIH provided humanitarian aid to over twenty countries, from Eastern and Central Europe to South America, in the form of medicine, medical supplies and equipment.

With the help of the well-known human rights activist Bianca Jagger, Harold voiced his anger against war crimes in Yugoslavia and set up projects to help the most affected victims of the civil war: the children. In 1994 ASIH became the first organization to remove seriously ill children from Bosnia for critical life-saving surgeries in the U.S.—where Harold worked very hard to get hospitals and surgeons to perform the operations free of charge. His extraordinary efforts at the time led to the establishment of the New York-Sarajevo Project, "Mosaic to Mosaic", by the then New York Mayor David Dinkins, and George Soros.

In 1998, Harold Robles retired from the Albert Schweitzer Institute for the Humanities and returned to his home country of the Netherlands to start work on a new approach. He wanted to find a way to focus completely on what he considered the most important part of his professional life: health education and information as a human right.

His many years spent working in public health made Harold realize that an enormous lack of basic health education, especially in poor countries, resulted in many unnecessary deaths. Inspired as always by Schweitzer, Harold was excited to work on an effective health education program fit for the twenty-first century. His commitment to public health and profound dedication to a country dear to his heart— South Africa—led him to create Health Promotion South Africa Trust

(HPSA) with his good friend, Dr. Jelle Braaksma, a well-known Dutch physician.

HPSA works to spread free health education to poor communities in Southern Africa. The idea of the "Health Promoter" is key to HPSA. A Health Promoter is someone from a township who receives basic health education, and who then goes on to teach more people this life-changing knowledge. This project provides much-needed jobs to people. Another thing that makes HPSA special is that attendees at the workshops are taught by people who speak the same language and who share similar living conditions and socio-economic backgrounds. This common ground makes it is much easier for Health Promoters to convey their important message. HPSA courses are based on the three pillars of "Mother and Child"; "Hygiene"; and "Healthy Lifestyle", and also celebrate the importance and joy of continued learning.

Of Harold's work with HPSA, Dr. S. A. Amos, Chief Director for Maternal, Child, Women's Health and Nutrition in the National Department of Health of South Africa, wrote:

> South Africa today boasts a reduction in maternal and infant mortality rates and has the highest number of patients on ARVs [medication] worldwide. The inspiration, motivation, persistence and perseverance gained from Dr. Robles' teachings in prevention in mother-to-child transmission [of HIV/AIDS] has left an indelible mark in my heart and continued to propel my team still in the helm of this program even today. Though our names will never appear in the annals of history . . . what Dr. Robles did for South Africa will remain immeasurable through eternity.

Harold Robles discussing the importance of health education with women in the townships of Southern Africa.

Harold has a very special connection with most of the children in the townships, who adore him and call him "Papa."

For my own part, I have enjoyed a thirty-year career working in many jobs rich with a dedication to development and civil service. But, I have never seen such a successful and passionate approach towards development than that practiced by my dear friend, Harold Robles. Harold has a unique way of involving everyone he meets in his mission to create a better world for the poor, and in particular for the children—the future generation. As Archbishop Desmond Tutu wrote to Harold in a letter from December 14, 2012:

> In the many years of our friendship I have witnessed and followed your dedication to improve matters in the right manner and not by trying to change people. Your mission of "Prevention through Education" is really making an impact on the many people that you touch in the townships across the nation. You are setting the stage for others to understand that cure is not always the answer to the problems that we are facing in underdeveloped countries. We in Africa are so thankful for the man who molded you so many years ago. Dr. Albert Schweitzer has instilled in you his philosophy of "Reverence for Life", and you are a living example of that philosophy.

Harold is passionate and charismatic. Much of his success stems from the fact that he is also honest and kind, and that he believes strongly in the goodness of people. Harold has shown that he has both the personality and energy to attract world leaders to his causes. These leaders include former U.S. Presidents, Jimmy Carter and Bill Clinton, as well as the former leader of the Soviet Union, Mikhail Gorbachev. In 2016, President Barack Obama honored Harold for his work, saying:

As you reflect on your achievements, I hope you take pride in the difference you have made in the lives of others. Congratulations on all you have accomplished. I wish you the very best in the years ahead as you continue working to forge an ever brighter tomorrow.

It all started with the sincere interest of an eight-year-old in the life and work of Dr. Albert Schweitzer. Now all grown up, Harold Robles has dedicated his life to serving others. By setting up the Health Promotion South Africa Trust, Harold has developed a lifelong mission that works hard to make Albert Schweitzer's philosophy of Reverence for Life a reality.

I hope reading about the life and work of Dr. Albert Schweitzer in this book has inspired you just as it inspired my dear friend Harold all those years ago. If this story of Schweitzer can teach you anything, it is that it can take *just one person* to make a big difference. I urge you to think about the ways in which you can care more for all of those around you (including the animals!) and go on your own journey of serving others by practicing a Reverence for Life.

Sources

"On one occasion. . . ." Albert Schweitzer, *Memoirs of Childhood and Youth* (New York: Macmillan, 1958), 2.

"The charm of. . . ." Ibid, 15.

"You don't deserve. . . ." Ibid, 40.

"A savior appeared. . . ." Ibid, 39.

"To me preaching. . . ." Albert Schweitzer, *Out of My Life and Thought* (New York: Holt, 1991), 25.

"I found on. . . ." Ibid, 85.

"Who can really. . . ." Albert Schweitzer, *On the Edge of the Primeval Forest* (London: A. & C. Black, 1956), 15.

"This man has. . . ." Ibid, 22.

"(L)eaning with all. . . ." Albert Schweitzer, *Out of My Life and Thought*, 154.

"As sunset of. . . ." Ibid, 155.

"Ever since the. . . ." Ibid, 185.

"I found for. . . ." Ibid, 186.

"What the world lacks. . . ." Albert Schweitzer, "Your Second Job," *Reader's Digest*, October 1949.

"On my visits. . . ." Albert Schweitzer, "Albert Schweitzer Speaks Out," *The 1964 World Book Year Book* (Field Enterprises Educational Corporation, 1964), 148.

"One of the transcendent. . . ." Norman Cousins, *Albert Schweitzer's Mission: Healing and Peace* (New York: Norton, 1985), 279.

"When I look. . . ." Albert Schweitzer, *Memoirs of Childhood and Youth*, 31.

Important Dates

1875	Born January 14 in Kayersberg, Alsace.
1885	Attends village school in Gunsbach and the Gymnasium in Mulhausen.
1893	Studies at the University of Strasbourg, with a year in military service.
1896	Decides that, when he is thirty, he will spend the rest of his life serving his fellow men and women.
1912	Marries Helene Bresslau.
1913	Dr. and Mrs. Schweitzer arrive in Africa.
1914-1917	The Schweitzers are considered enemy aliens by French authorities and placed under house arrest. Later they are deported to France as prisoners of war.
1919	The Schweitzer's only child, Rhena, is born on January 14.
1924-1927	Returns to Africa and rebuilds hospital.
1928-1939	Makes several trips to and from Africa. Lectures widely and gives organ concerts throughout Europe.
1939-1948	Remains in Africa during World War II.
1949	Makes first and only trip to the United States.
1952	Awarded the Nobel Peace Prize.
1955	Receives the Order of Merit from Queen Elizabeth II in London.
1957	Helene Schweitzer dies in Zurich, Switzerland, on June 1.
1958-1963	Works for Limited Test Ban Treaty. Expands the hospital in Lambaréné.
1965	Dies at the age of ninety in Lambaréné on September 4.

Further Reading

BY ALBERT SCHWEITZER

Schweitzer, Albert, Jimmy Carter (Foreword), Lachlan Forrow (Preface), and Rhena Schweitzer Miller (Preface). *Out of My Life and Thought: An Autobiography.* Translated by Antje Bultmann Lemke. Baltimore, MD: The Johns Hopkins University Press, 2009.

Schweitzer, Albert. *Peace or Atomic War?* London: Black, 1958.

Schweitzer, Albert, and William Foege (Foreword). *The Primeval Forest.* Baltimore, MD: The Johns Hopkins University Press, 1998.

Schweitzer, Albert. *Memoirs of Childhood and Youth.* New York, NY: Macmillan, 1958.

Schweitzer, Albert, and Jaroslav Pelikan (Foreword). *The Mysticism of Paul the Apostle.* Baltimore, MD: The Johns Hopkins University Press, 1998.

Schweitzer, Albert, and Delbert Hillers (Foreword). *The Quest of the Historical Jesus: A Critical Study of Its Progress from Reimarus to Wrede.* Baltimore, MD: The Johns Hopkins University Press in association with the Albert Schweitzer Institute, 1998.

Schweitzer, Albert. *Reverence for Life: The Words of Albert Schweitzer.* Edited by Harold Robles. Anna Maria, FL: Maurice Bassett, 2017.

ABOUT ALBERT SCHWEITZER

Barsam, Ara Paul. *Reverence for Life: Albert Schweitzer's Great Contribution to Ethical Thought.* Oxford: Oxford University Press, 2008.

Bentley, James. *Albert Schweitzer: The Doctor Who Devoted His Life to Africa's Sick*. Milwaukee, WI: Gareth Stevens, 1991.

– *Albert Schweitzer: The Doctor Who Gave Up a Brilliant Career to Serve the People of Africa*. Milwaukee, WI: Gareth Stevens, 1991.

Brabazon, James. *Albert Schweitzer: A Biography*. Second edition. Syracuse, NY: Syracuse University Press, 2000.

Crawford, Gail. *Albert Schweitzer*. Morristown, NJ: Silver Burdett, 1990.

Johnson, Spencer. *The Value of Dedication: The Story of Albert Schweitzer*. Stamford, CT.: Oak Tree, 1979.

Schweitzer, Albert, and Helene Bresslau. *The Albert Schweitzer-Helene Bresslau Letters, 1902-1912*. Edited by Rhena Schweitzer Miller, Gustav Woytt, and Nancy Stewart (Associate Editor). Translated by Antje Bultmann. Lemke. Syracuse, NY: Syracuse University Press, 2003.

ABOUT AFRICA

Jones, Constance. *A Short History of Africa*. New York: Facts on File, 1993.

Perryman, Andrew. *Gabon*. New York: Chelsea House, 1988.

ABOUT THE MEDICAL PROFESSION

Aaseng, Nathan. *The Disease Fighters: The Nobel Prize in Medicine*. Minneapolis, MN: Lerner, 1987.

Curtis, Robert H. *Great Lives: Medicine*. New York: Macmillan, 1992.

Epstein, Rachel. *Careers in Health Care*. New York: Chelsea House, 1989.

There are many more books by and about Albert Schweitzer. Contact your local library, or:

The Albert Schweitzer Institute for the Humanities at Quinnipiac University in Hamden, Connecticut:

www.qu.edu/on-campus/institutes-centers/albert-schweitzer-institute.html

Maison Albert Schweitzer: Archives Centrales in Gunsbach, France:

https://www.schweitzer.org/en/archives/

Index

Page numbers in **bold** refer to illustrations.

Albert Schweitzer Center (Netherlands), 63, 85
Albert Schweitzer Institute for the Humanities (ASIH), 63–64, 85
Albert Schweitzer Youth Club, 63
Alsace, 18, 22, 37, 71
Amos, S.A., 65
animals, 17, 25, 39, 48, **49**, 54, 58, 68
ASIH (Albert Schweitzer Institute for the Humanities), 63–64, 85
atomic bomb, 55, 56
Azvawami, Joseph, 34

Bach, Johann Sebastian, 22, 37, 41, 58, 61
Braaksma, Jelle, 65

Catholic Church, 29–30
Central African Republic, 29
Chad, 29
Congo, 29, 33
Congo Mission, 29–30
Cousins, Norman, 56, 63

"Declaration of Conscience," 56
Dinkins, David, 64

Elizabeth II, Queen of England, 58, 71

Franz Ferdinand, Archduke of Austria-Hungary, 32
French Equatorial Africa, 29

Gabon, 29, 33, 37
Garaison prison, 42
Gillespie, Noel, 47–48

Goethe, Johann Wolfgang von, 52
Gunsbach, Alsace, 18, **19**, 20, 25, 30, 43, **44**, 71
Gymnasium (secondary school), 20-21, 71

Haakon, King of Norway, 55
Health Promoter, 65, 81–82, 85
Health Promotion South Africa Trust (HPSA), 64–65, 68, 81-82, 86
Hitler, Adolf, 50
HPSA (Health Promotion South Africa Trust), 64–65, 68, 81-82, 86

Jagger, Bianca, 64

Kaysersberg, Alsace, 18, 71
Kennedy, John F., president of U.S., 57

Lambaréné, 33–37, **35**, **36**, **38**, 43, 46, 48, 50, **51**, **55**, 56, **57**, 58, **59**, 60, 61, **62**, 63, 71
leprosy, 36, 52, 54, 56
Limited Test Ban Treaty, 57, 71

Mendelssohn, Felix, 20, 37
"Mosaic to Mosaic", 64
Münch, Eugen, 20
museum in Lambaréné, 61
music, 13, 19–22, 25, 27, 37, 41, **45**, **51**, 61

Nobel Peace Prize, 54-56, 71
nuclear war / nuclear weapons, 14, 24, 55-57

Obama, Barack, president of U.S., 67–68, 86
Ogowe River, 33, 34, **40**
On the Edge of the Primeval Forest (Schweitzer), 46

Paris, France, 22, 25, 30, 31
Paris Bach Society, 31, 37

Paris Missionary Society, 29, 34

Peace or Atomic War? (Schweitzer), 56

Philosophy of Civilization (Schweitzer), 38–39

prison camps, 41, 42, 71

Reverence for Life philosophy, 12, 13–14, 18, 20, 30, 39–41, **40**, 46, 50, 54, 56, 61, 63, 67, 68

Robles, Harold E., 13, 14, 61–68, **66**, **85**, 85–86

St. Nicholas Church, Strasbourg, 27

Saint-Sulpice Church, Paris, 22, 31

Schweitzer, Adele Schillinger, 18, **19**, 43

Schweitzer, Albert, **14**, **16**, **23**, **26**, **31**, **36**, **38**, **44**, **45**, **47**, **49**, **51**, **53**, **59**, 60

in Africa, 33–41, 47–48, 50–51, 58–60

animals and, 17, 25, 39, 48, **49**, 54, 58, 68

birth of, 18, 71

birth of daughter, 43, 71

childhood of, 17–22

death of, 60, 71

education of, 19-22, **23**, 24

first voyage to Africa, 32–33

Helene Bresslau and, **28**, 28–31, **31**, 32, 33, **36**, 37, **38**, 39, 42, 43, 46, 48, 51-52, 54-55, 58, 71

house arrest of, 37–39, **38**

Jesus and, 13

as lecturer, 46, 52–54, **53**

medical studies of, 30

military service and, 22, 24

music and, 13, 19–22, 25, 27, 37, 41, **45**, **51**, 61

Nobel Peace Prize awarded to, 54, 71

nuclear war / nuclear weapons, 14, 55–57

On the Edge of the Primeval Forest, 46

Peace or Atomic War?, 56

Philosophy of Civilization, 38–39

preaching and, 27

in prison camps, 41, 42, 71

Reverence for Life philosophy, 12, 13–14, 18, 20, 30, 39-41, **40**, 46, 50, 54, 56, 61, 63, 67, 68

visit to U.S., 52-54, **53**

world fame and honors, 50, 54–56

World War I and, 32, 37, 41-43, 71

World War II and, 50, 52, 55, 71

Schweitzer, Julie Adele, **19**

Schweitzer, Louis, 18, **19**, 30

Schweitzer, Louise, **19**

Schweitzer, Margerit, **19**

Schweitzer, Paul, **19**

Schweitzer, Rhena, 13–14, **14**, 43, **44**, 46, 50, 51–52, 63, 71

Schweitzer-Bresslau, Helene, **28**, 28–31, **31**, 32, 33, **36**, 37, **38**, 39, 42, 43, 46, 48, 58, 71

Schweitzer family, **19**

Soderblom, Nathan, 46

Sorbonne University, 25

Soros, George, 64

Tutu, Desmond, 67

Uppsala University, 46

University of Strasbourg, 22, **23**, 24, 25, 29, 71

Wehmann, Doctor, 21

Widor, Charles-Marie, 22, 25, 37, 39, 41

World War I, 32, 37, 41-43, 71

World War II, 50, 52, 55, 71

A Call to Action

HOW CAN I SUPPORT THE LIFE-CHANGING HEALTH EDUCATION ACTIVITIES OF THE HEALTH PROMOTERS?

Are you aware of the number of people dying unnecessarily due to a lack of basic health knowledge? Many of these people would still be alive today had their mother, father, caregiver or healthcare worker known what to do to provide the necessary care to them, as well as when and where to seek professional help.

Millions of children under the age of five years old are st7ill dying of preventable diseases such as diarrhea, measles, malaria, and pneumonia, to name just a few. But the lack of relevant and reliable healthcare information available to healthcare providers in vulnerable and low-resource settings means this vicious cycle of avoidable death continues.

WHY IS HEALTH EDUCATION SO IMPORTANT?

Because, simply put, it saves lives. For those of us in a position to help our fellow man, it is important that we invest in health education to foster care to those less fortunate than us.

Life Changing Health Education is the mission and goal of the Health Promotion South Africa Trust (HPSA), a South African organization with supporting organizations in Europe and the United States of America.

With highly trained facilitators, the Health Promoters are focusing with full conviction on their objective to improve the living conditions of the population in Southern Africa by giving health related training and workshops in their local communities.

Health Promoters offer Basic Health Education workshops at a very easy-to-understand, grass-roots level. The workshops aim at giving relevant, practical and above all preventative advice to non-professional audiences.

Among the chosen workshops, priority has been given to practical health issues such as childhood diseases and immunizations, family planning, female hygiene, oral health, primary HIV/AIDS care, addiction and mental health, sanitation and other chronic lifestyle diseases. These workshops are conducted in an array of local languages, which take into consideration certain cultural differences and adapt accordingly to deliver the important messages of health education in an informal, everyday manner.

The Health Promoters' passion lies in imparting vital knowledge and caring wholeheartedly for their communities. With your support, the Health Promoters will be able to spearhead dynamic change in the local communities of Africa, and even beyond the borders of Africa. Get involved in the fight to promote basic health education today!

JOIN THE HEALTH PROMOTERS COMMUNITY

Website:	www.healthpromoters.co.za
Facebook:	www.facebook.com/TheHealthPromoters
Twitter:	www.twitter.com/HealthPromoters
YouTube:	www.youtube.com/HealthPromoters
Instagram:	www.instagram.com/healthpromotersofficial

HPSA received the approval of Barack Obama in 2016. HPSA has been affiliated with the United Nations since 9 May 2019.

Order your bracelets

Wear the change you want to see.

Buy Health Promoter Bracelets online and help build a better and healthier future for all.

when you buy these bracelets you donate to Health Promoters Life Changing Health Education and create jobs for people in low income communities.

vist our webiste today

www.relate.org.za

Relate
100% NOT-FOR-PROFIT
www.relate.org.za

If you do not have access to a QR code scanner, please visit
https://www.relate.org.za/shop/health-promoters-trust

About the Author

Dr. Harold E. Robles is well known for his international humanitarian work. He became a devotee of Albert Schweitzer at the age of eight, and in 1973 he founded the Albert Schweitzer Center in the Netherlands. Two years later, he was appointed Secretary General of the International Schweitzer Organization (ASIL), an organization founded by Dr. Schweitzer in the 1930s in Strasbourg, France.

In 1981, Robles immigrated to the United States where together with Rhena Schweitzer Miller, the daughter of Dr. Schweitzer, he founded the Albert Schweitzer Institute for the Humanities (ASIH), an organization dedicated to the philosophy of Albert Schweitzer. In 1998, at the age of fifty, he retired from the Institute and was given the title

President Emeritus.

In 1999, Dr. Robles founded the Medical Knowledge Institute Trust, an international non-profit organization that focuses on offering education and information, grounded in the conviction that health education is a human right. In 2013 he and the trustees changed the name of the organization to Health Promotion South Africa Trust (HPSA).

In September 2008, Dr. Robles was inducted for a period of two years into The Third Chamber, otherwise known as the shadow parliament for international cooperation in the Netherlands. Its 150 members work on political and public support for international cooperation.

Dr. Robles has received significant recognition for his work. On 29 April 2009, Queen Beatrix of the Netherlands granted him a Knighthood, "Ridder in de Orde van Oranje Nassau." In 2012 he was named "Outstanding African Personality for Health Advocacy," and in November 2016 President Barack Obama honored Dr. Robles and HPSA. It was also a great honor for him to be one of 500 Dutch citizens invited to attend the coronation of King Willem-Alexander of the Netherlands on 30 April 2013 in Amsterdam.

Robles has written several books about Albert Schweitzer, published in the Netherlands, former East Germany, Italy, China, Korea, former Yugoslavia and the United States.

He is Goodwill Ambassador of the Ethnic Business Women Society of the Netherlands and Goodwill Representative of the Southern Africa/Netherlands Chamber of Commerce (SANEC).

Also available by Albert Schweitzer
Edited by Harold E. Robles

I cannot but have reverence for all that is called life. I cannot avoid compassion for everything that is called life. That is the beginning and foundation of morality.

Albert Schweitzer

MAURICE BASSETT

Gathered together for the first time in one place are Nobel Peace Prize-winner Albert Schweitzer's words on ecology, human and animal rights, philosophy, war and peace, music and the arts, and forming a global community.

"The words of Dr. Schweitzer are timeless. They are not only relevant today, but they will continue to serve as an inspiration to the future. Many thanks to Harold Robles for compiling and sharing with us this collection of '*Le Grand Docteur's*' thoughts."
Former President Jimmy Carter

"If you are a thinker, if you care about the future of this planet, you need to buy this little gem of a book."
Jane Goodall

Available in both paperback and audiobook formats on Amazon.com

Notes

Notes

Notes

Notes

Notes

Notes

Notes

Notes

Publisher's Catalogue

The Prosperous Series

#1 The Prosperous Coach: Increase Income and Impact for You and Your Clients (Steve Chandler and Rich Litvin)

#2 The Prosperous Hip Hop Producer: My Beat-Making Journey from My Grandma's Patio to a Six-Figure Business (Curtiss King)

#3 The Prosperous Hotelier (David Lund)

* * *

Devon Bandison

Fatherhood Is Leadership: Your Playbook for Success, Self-Leadership, and a Richer Life

Roy G. Biv

Dancing on Rainbows: A Celebration of Numismatic Art

Sir Fairfax L. Cartwright

The Mystic Rose from the Garden of the King

Steve Chandler

37 Ways to BOOST Your Coaching Practice: PLUS: the 17 Lies That Hold Coaches Back and the Truth That Sets Them Free

50 Ways to Create Great Relationships

Business Coaching (Steve Chandler and Sam Beckford)

Crazy Good: A Book of CHOICES

CREATOR

Death Wish: The Path through Addiction to a Glorious Life

Fearless: Creating the Courage to Change the Things You Can

How to Get Clients (Revised Edition)

The Prosperous Coach: Increase Income and Impact for You and Your Clients (The Prosperous Series #1) (Steve Chandler and Rich Litvin)

RIGHT NOW: Mastering the Beauty of the Present Moment

Shift Your Mind Shift The World (Revised Edition)

Time Warrior: How to defeat procrastination, people-pleasing, self-doubt, over-commitment, broken promises and chaos

Wealth Warrior: The Personal Prosperity Revolution

Kazimierz Dąbrowski

Positive Disintegration

Charles Dickens

A Christmas Carol: A Special Full-Color, Fully-Illustrated Edition

Melissa Ford

Living Service: The Journey of a Prosperous Coach

James F. Gesualdi

Excellence Beyond Compliance: Enhancing Animal Welfare Through the Constructive Use of the Animal Welfare Act

Janice Goldman

Let's Talk About Money: The Girlfriends' Guide to Protecting Her ASSets

Sylvia Hall

This Is Real Life: Love Notes to Wake You Up

Christy Harden

Guided by Your Own Stars: Connect with the Inner Voice and Discover Your Dreams

I ♥ Raw: A How-To Guide for Reconnecting to Yourself and the Earth through Plant-Based Living

Curtiss King

The Prosperous Hip Hop Producer: My Beat-Making Journey from My Grandma's Patio to a Six-Figure Business (The Prosperous Series #2)

David Lindsay

A Blade for Sale: The Adventures of Monsieur de Mailly

David Lund

The Prosperous Hotelier (The Prosperous Series #3)

Abraham H. Maslow

The Aims of Education (audio)

The B-language Workshop (audio)

Being Abraham Maslow (DVD)

The Eupsychian Ethic (audio)

The Farther Reaches of Human Nature (audio)

Maslow and Self-Actualization (DVD)

Maslow on Management (audiobook)

Personality and Growth: A Humanistic Psychologist in the Classroom

Psychology and Religious Awareness (audio)

The Psychology of Science: A Reconnaissance

Self-Actualization (audio)

Weekend with Maslow (audio)

Harold E. Robles

Albert Schweitzer: An Adventurer for Humanity

Albert Schweitzer

Reverence for Life: The Words of Albert Schweitzer

William Tillier

Personality Development through Positive Disintegration: The Work of Kazimierz Dąbrowski

Margery Williams

The Velveteen Rabbit: or How Toys Become Real

Join our Mailing List:
www.MauriceBassett.com

MAURICE BASSETT

books for athletes of the mind

Made in the USA
Columbia, SC
25 August 2020